THE NATURE KIDS GUIDE TO
FOXES

DAVID ANDERSON

LP Media Inc. Publishing

For information address LP Media Inc. Publishing,
30012 Variolite St NW, Princeton MN 55371
www.lpmedia.org

Publication Data

Foxes
The Nature Kid's Guide to Foxes — First edition.

Summary: "Learn all about Foxes, the Nature Kid Way"
— Provided by publisher.

ISBN: 979-8-89818-097-3

[1. Foxes – Non-Fiction] I. Title.

Title: The Nature Kid's Guide to Foxes

CONTENTS

Forest Friends 4

Foxes Everywhere 6

Small Stuff 8

Fluffy Features 10

Super Senses 12

Tricky Tails 14

Hungry Hunters 16

Pounce Time 18

Watch Out 20

Quick Escape 22

Fast Feet 24

Night Life 26

Lone Rangers 28

Finding Friends 30

Cute Kits 32

Family First 34

Fantastic Fox Survival . . . 36

Spotting Sneaky Foxes . . 38

FOREST FRIENDS

Yip! A red fox peeks out from the bushes. Its orange fur glows bright.

Foxes live in many places around the world. They make homes in forests, grasslands, and mountains. Some foxes even live in deserts or snowy tundras.

Forests are great homes for foxes. Tall trees give them shade, and thick bushes help them hide. Fallen logs make good spots to rest too.

Foxes dig dens underground. These dens have tunnels and rooms. The dens keep foxes safe from bad weather and protect them from other animals.

DID YOU KNOW

Tibetan sand foxes live high in the mountains of China and have square-shaped faces.

FOXES EVERYWHERE

Rustle! A gray fox runs through dry leaves. It looks for food.

Foxes live on almost every continent. They are found in North America, Europe, Asia, Africa, and Australia. Only Antarctica has no foxes.

Red foxes have the biggest range. They live in more places than any other wild meat-eating animal. Arctic foxes live only in cold northern lands.

Fennec foxes live in African deserts. Gray foxes live in American forests.

Red foxes often live in cities in many parts of the world. They find food near people.

SMALL STUFF

Snap! A tiny fennec fox jumps on a twig. Its big ears catch every sound.

Foxes are small to medium-sized animals. Many weigh about the same as house cats. Some weigh just five or six pounds.

Red foxes are are the biggest. They can weigh up to fifteen pounds. Their long, bushy tails add extra length.

Fennec foxes are the smallest of all. They only weigh about three pounds!

Red foxes stand about 16 inches at the shoulder. That is knee-high to an adult.

FLUFFY FEATURES

Fox fur has two layers. A soft undercoat traps heat and keeps foxes cozy.

Swoosh! A fox's fluffy tail swings behind it as it runs.

Foxes have thick, soft fur. This fur keeps them warm in cold weather. It also helps them stay cool when it gets hot.

Fox fur comes in many colors. Red foxes have orange or reddish coats. Arctic foxes have white fur in winter and brown fur in summer.

Foxes have pointed ears and long snouts. Their whiskers help them feel things around them. Sharp claws help them dig dens.

A fox's legs are thin but strong. Soft pads on their feet help them walk quietly.

12

Crunch! A red fox hears a mouse under the snow. It leaps high and dives in.

Foxes hear high sounds people miss. Their ears rotate to find where sounds come from. This helps them hunt even when their prey is hiding.

Foxes also have a strong sense of smell. They can smell food buried under ground. This helps them eat in winter.

Fox eyes see well in low light too. This lets them hunt at night.

TRICKY
TAILS

Whoosh! A red fox waves its bushy tail. It confuses a hungry coyote.

Foxes use their tails in clever ways. A fox can wave its tail to distract predators. This gives it time to run away.

Fox tails have a white tip. This helps kits follow their mother in tall grass. The bright spot is easy to see.

Some foxes puff up their tails. This makes them look bigger and scarier. A puffed tail may deter some predators.

A fox's tail is called a brush. Foxes wrap their tails around them to stay warm.

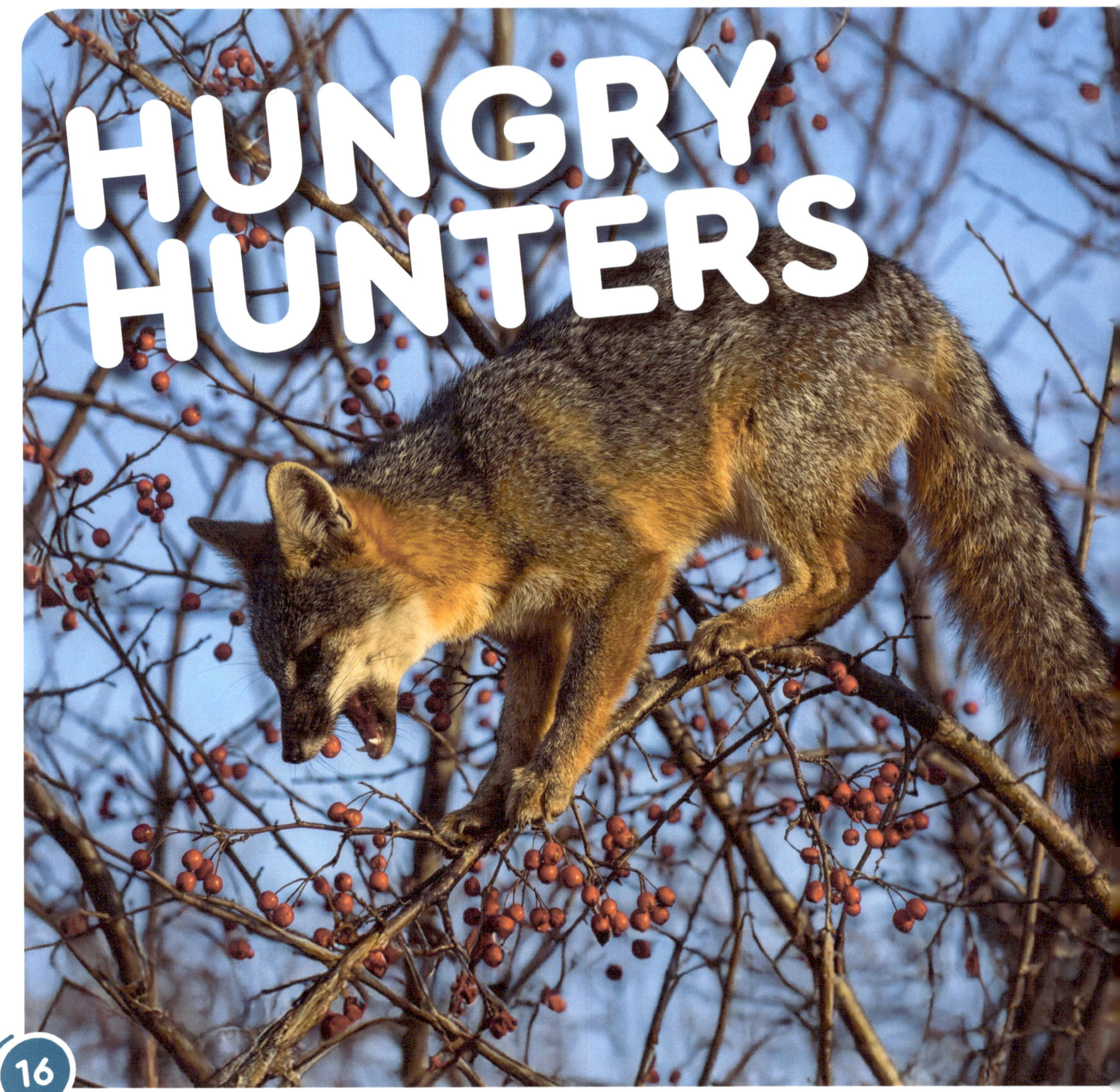

HUNGRY
HUNTERS
16

Chomp! A gray fox bites into a juicy berry. It loves this sweet treat.

Foxes eat many kinds of food. They are **omnivores**, which means they eat both plants and animals.

Foxes hunt mice, rabbits, and birds. They also catch insects and frogs. But small prey can be hard to find in some places.

Foxes enjoy fruits and berries too. They munch on apples and grapes. Foxes will even scavenge through trash when hungry.

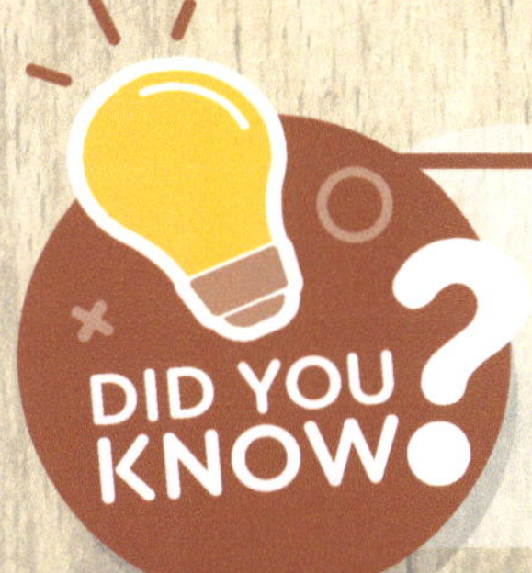

A fox will eat about 1 to 2 pounds of food a day.

POUNCE TIME

Foxes can pounce up to 12 feet forward. They catch prey 75% of the time facing north.

18

Thump! A red fox lands on the snow. It caught a vole!

Foxes have a special way to catch prey. They use a move called mousing. This hunting trick helps them find food hidden under the snow.

The fox listens carefully for tiny sounds. Voles and mice move in tunnels below the surface. A fox can hear these small animals from far away. Its big ears help it pinpoint the exact spot.

When ready, the fox leaps high into the air. This pounce can reach three feet up! The fox dives down headfirst into the snow. Its sharp nose breaks through to grab the prey below.

WATCH OUT

Growl! A coyote spots a fox. The fox must act fast.

Foxes face many dangers in the wild. Larger animals hunt them for food. That is why foxes must always stay alert.

Coyotes and wolves chase foxes across open fields. Eagles swoop down from above. Even big owls hunt small foxes at night.

Young foxes face the most risk of all. Kits are small and cannot run fast yet. They stay close to their dens for safety.

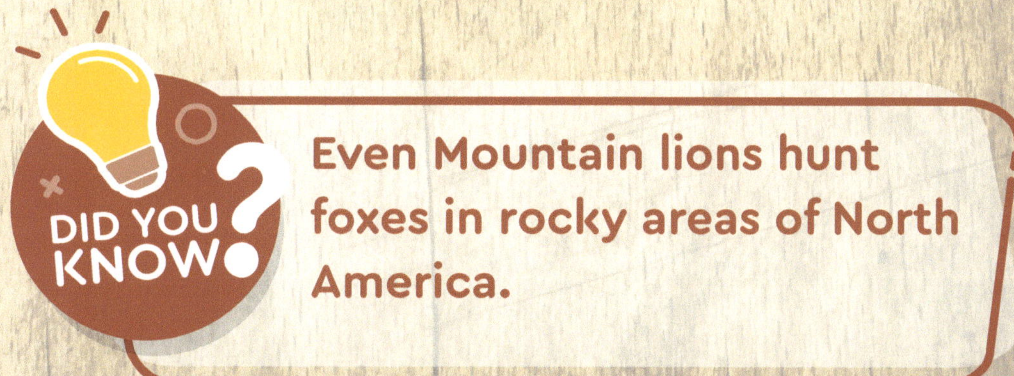

QUICK
ESCAPE

Screech! A kit fox darts into a hole and vanishes in a flash.

Foxes can escape danger well. They use speed and smarts to stay safe.

Foxes know their home area well. They remember many dens and hiding spots. This helps them escape quickly.

Foxes squeeze into tight spaces. Their slim bodies fit into small holes. Bigger animals cannot follow them inside.

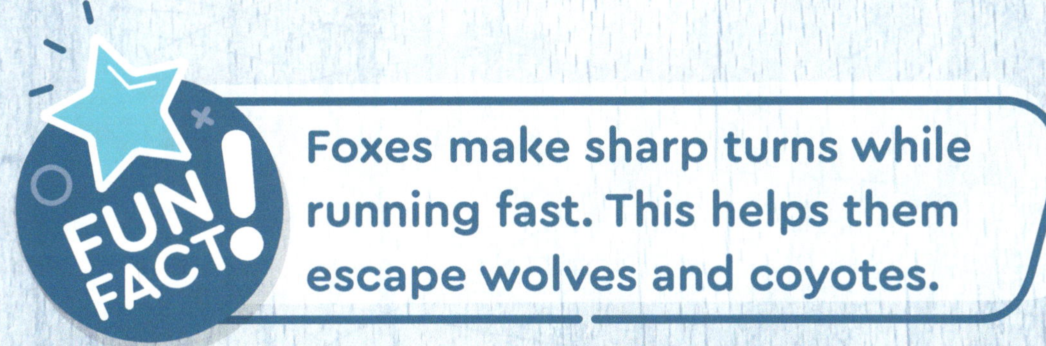

FAST FEET

24

Zoom! A swift fox races across the prairie at night.

Long legs help foxes move quickly. This speed helps them cover lots of ground.

Red foxes can run up to 30 miles per hour. That is faster than most dogs!

Foxes can travel up to 5 miles each night. They search for food, water, and safe places to rest.

Arctic foxes travel over 2,000 miles in a single year searching for food across the tundra.

NIGHT LIFE

Howl! A red fox calls out in the dark. Above, stars shine in the night sky.

Foxes are **nocturnal**. This means they are active at night. They sleep during the day.

When the sun is out, foxes rest in shady spots or dens. They curl up and wrap their tails around their bodies. Their fluffy tails keep them warm.

At dusk, foxes wake up. They stretch and start to move. The cool night air helps them hunt.

A fox's eyes have a special layer that reflects light. This helps them see well in the dark.

LONE RANGERS

Click! A gray fox walks alone. It sniffs the cold air.

Most foxes live alone. They do not form packs like wolves do.

Foxes hunt by themselves. Hunting solo helps them catch small prey.

Each fox has its own **territory**. They mark the edges with scent. This tells other foxes to stay away.

Foxes only gather together during mating season.

A red fox's territory can cover up to 5 square miles. Males have bigger areas.

FINDING FRIENDS

Bark! A red fox calls into the night. This sound means it wants a mate.

Foxes mate once a year. This happens in winter for most **species**.

Male foxes make loud barking sounds. Female foxes answer with screams. These calls travel far in the cold air.

Foxes also use scent to find each other. They leave special smells on rocks and trees. Other foxes follow these scent trails.

Arctic foxes mate between February and April when snow still covers the ground in their **habitat**.

CUTE KITS

Fox kits stay in the den for about one month. Then they start to explore the world outside with their mother.

Squeak! Tiny fox babies wiggle in a den. They cannot see yet.

Baby foxes are called kits. A mother fox has four to six of these tiny babies.

Fox kits are born with eyes closed. They cannot hear yet either. Their ears open after about two weeks. Their eyes open soon after.

Fox kits drink mother's milk first. Later, parents bring meat to the kits. This helps them learn to eat solid food.

Fox kits play and wrestle together. This helps them grow strong.

FAMILY FIRST

A mother fox guards her den. Her kits play inside.

Fox parents work together. Both the mother and father care for their young.

The mother stays with her kits in the den. She keeps them warm and safe. Meanwhile, the father brings food to the family.

Fox families stay together for several months. The kits learn to hunt by watching their parents. They practice by catching bugs and mice.

By fall, young foxes leave home to find their own territories.

Older fox sisters sometimes help raise new kits in the den.

SURVIVORS

Rustle! A red fox hides behind a garden shed.

Foxes have many ways to survive in cities. They are not picky eaters. A fox will munch on berries, bugs, or leftover pizza. They find food in parks, yards, and trash cans.

Foxes are clever and brave. They learn to cross busy streets. They know which neighbors leave food outside.

Foxes make dens in surprising places. They dig under porches and sheds. Some even raise babies in backyards!

FOX
SPOTTING

Rustle! A red fox darts behind a bush. It hears kids playing nearby.

Foxes are hard to spot. They hide during the day. Most foxes come out at dawn and dusk. This is the best time to look for them.

Watch for movement near fields and forests. Foxes hunt in open areas. They walk slowly and stop often. Their ears turn to catch sounds.

Look for fox tracks in mud or snow. Fox prints show four toes. The prints form a straight line when foxes walk.

Foxes are easiest to track in winter. Look for their footprints in mud or snow.

GLOSSARY

omnivores
Animals that eat both plants and meat.

nocturnal
Active at night and sleeping during the day.

species
A group of animals that are the same kind.

territory
An area of land that an animal lives in and protects as its own.

habitats
Places where animals live and find food and shelter.